VERANDA
Elements of Beauty
THE ART OF DECORATING

KATHRYN O'SHEA-EVANS

FOREWORD BY
STEELE THOMAS MARCOUX

CONTENTS

FOREWORD 6

INTRODUCTION 8

CHAPTER ONE
Living Rooms 12

CHAPTER TWO
Sunrooms 60

CHAPTER THREE
Gardens 78

CHAPTER FOUR
Dining Rooms 110

CHAPTER FIVE
Kitchens 146

CHAPTER SIX
Breakfast Rooms 160

CHAPTER SEVEN
Bedrooms 178

CHAPTER EIGHT
Baths 218

CHAPTER NINE
Passages 236

INDEX 266

PHOTOGRAPHY CREDITS 271

OPPOSITE: Legend Albert Hadley (and his team at Parish-Hadley) designed this timeless North Carolina living room in the 1970s. He later updated it for modern living with just one trick: he had the previous apricot walls painted a glazed pea green.

FOREWORD

"Decorating is not about making stage sets, it's not about making pretty pictures for the magazines; it's really about creating a quality of life, a beauty that nourishes the soul." So said famed American interior designer Albert Hadley, who was known as much for designing spaces with intellectual rigor as with au courant urbanity. Hadley had a certain finesse when it came to decorating that cemented his legacy as one of the greatest designers of the 20th century. His historically informed yet elegantly fashionable approach yielded rooms with warmth, personality, and a certain permanence that make them nearly impossible to date. In other words, they are inviting, unique, and timeless.

This, I believe, is the true art of decorating: creating livable spaces that magnetically draw others in even while closely reflecting their owners' individual points of view. These are the rooms that leave a lasting impression on us, where we celebrate the joys of life and seek comfort during times of sorrow. These are the rooms we just want to be in—because, thanks to an enthralling combination of sensory stimulants from color and pattern to texture, fragrance, and sound, these rooms feel as beautiful as they look.

This book, organized by room type into nine magnificent chapters, distills the process of creating these spaces down to its elements. With expert insights culled from top designers, architects, and landscape architects from all over the world, no detail of design, from choosing the right occasional chairs and lighting fixtures to navigating the myriad options of kitchen backsplash surfaces, has been overlooked. And, with unexpected decorating ideas like tenting a breakfast room ceiling, its pages are filled with a kind of originality Mr. Hadley likely would have admired.

Beyond all of the beautiful decorative aspirations, this book is meant to inspire a wholly beautiful way of living—with ideas for engaging the auditory and olfactory senses, in addition to sight and touch. The rooms featured in the pages to come are infused with a heady concoction of personal style and gracious design, where the whole is more enchanting, more memorable, than the sum of its parts could ever be. May we all discover and perpetuate that soul-nourishing beauty at home.

STEELE THOMAS MARCOUX

INTRODUCTION

Our innate desire for beauty is every bit as powerful as our yearning for love and happiness. Our bodies may thrive with the latest wellness trends, but it's beauty that truly satisfies our souls. You don't have to look much further than history for proof. Claude Monet knew that surrounding himself with exultant gardens and the Normandy light at Giverny would soothe his worries. Thomas Jefferson designed Monticello in elegant symmetry for a calming respite from politics. Today, New Yorkers crave over-the-top splendor so much that they'll willingly wait in line for hours (in high heels) to see the latest Costume Institute exhibition at The Met. But a beautiful life doesn't require a private estate or an invitation to an exclusive event, as anyone who has woken up to a simple bedside bouquet of fragrant lilac cuttings from the garden can attest. It just requires an observant eye that's open to finding and appreciating the beauty in design and in daily living.

In researching this book, we spoke with interior designers, architects, and landscape designers about how they introduce elements of beauty into the spaces they design so lovingly. Their special touches can be found in many surprising places: the intricate shadows cast by a chandelier on a dining room ceiling; the exuberant foliage of a well-tended flower garden; the sense of balance experienced when strolling by a gallery wall arranged in simple symmetry. Often, it's those moments that bring loveliness to your hours—and with it, to your spirit.

OPPOSITE: Arrange ranunculus and snapdragons in an unexpected, multi-tiered way to capitalize on their feral beauty. Placing them in a collection of pottery in a limited palette allows their hues to pop.

PAGE 7: Hadley used his signature florals to sweeten the bedrooms of this 1970s North Carolina project, which proves good design holds up: that bed looks every bit as divinely restful today.

This stunning collection of photographs and designer insights reveals instructive, exquisite rooms that depict beauty from morning to night while pushing the gold-leafed envelope on design rules. There is a breakfast room sheathed in Swedish paneling with birdcage pendant lamps over the table and a cosseting master bedroom where gilded moldings echo the finish of the bed corona made from an antique French altar fragment. Organized by room, each chapter displays those special details that make a room arresting and remind readers that some of the most beauteous thrills can happen anywhere, in any corner of the house. Throughout, designers share personal advice for creating delightful environments, whether that's how to make your fresh-cut flowers last longer, which antique chairs are so timeless they're worth hunting for, or the art of properly dressing a bed so beautifully that it invites you to sink into it with a happy sigh at the end of a busy day.

OPPOSITE: Megawatt silent film star Mary Pickford once owned this Georgian armchair; no wonder Richard Keith Langham gave it pride of place before a showstopping circa-1900 crewel panel backdrop in this 19th century farmhouse in Lancaster County, Pennsylvania.

CHAPTER ONE

Living Rooms

This is the one place in the house that is truly meant and dedicated for Living, with a capital L,

whether that means hosting a crowd for cocktail hour, splaying out on the rug with the kids and a basket of heirloom toys, or curling up fireside with a glass of port and your dog-eared Flannery O'Connor. Long called the *parlor*—from the French word *parler*, i.e., "to speak," owing to the abundance of chitchat that often happens there—there's a reason we now call these spaces *living* rooms. To create for a setting in which memorable scenes can unfold, act the movie director and whip up a set that can command attention. Billowing sheer white curtains hung from ceiling to floor for a seraphic approach create a de facto art installation whenever there's a breeze. Vintage Louis XV chairs upholstered in butter yellow bring indoors all the joy of a sunny afternoon. Vast collections of books that stack to the rafters can turn a living room into a library—a studious ode to art that inspires nights off from Netflix. (In their place? Binge-reading.) Even something as simple as a ceiling—gilded in, say, silver leaf and gold Venetian wax—can delight your eyes as you linger on the divan. Whatever you choose, just remember: This is a room that was tailor-made for seizing the day in every way.

PAGES 12-13: An eye-catching mirror by Hervé Van der Straeten glimmers as a focal point in a Charlotte, North Carolina, home designed by Betsy Brown.

OPPOSITE: Inject energy into an otherwise buttoned-up room by going wild with upholstery, such as on these yellow leather Louis XV chairs in decorator Juan Pablo Molyneux's château, 30 miles south of Paris in Pouy-sur-Vannes. "I don't have a style. I have a lifestyle," the designer says.

ABOVE: Utilize varying textures for a warm effect, such as in this Palm Beach living room by Phoebe Howard.

RIGHT: Throw pillows in this Palm Beach sitting room designed by Betsy Shiverick "draw the eye to the adjacent art."

ABOVE: Intricate carved moldings draw the eye skyward in this Sag Harbor, New York, 1801 whaling captain's house designed by Sharon Simonaire.

LEFT: Stunning pieces are everywhere you look in Hutton Wilkinson's Malibu home—such as this chest used on the set of the film *My Fair Lady*. "All houses should be arranged for the pleasure of the owner and nobody else," Wilkinson says. "I think we all have a personal palette. Whatever catches our eyes will go together with anything else we have collected. It really frees me to do things that are vibrant and interesting."

LIVING ROOMS **17**

ABOVE: A Manhattan library designed by Ellie Cullman and architect John B. Murray is paneled in polished French anigre wood. "Today we're always talking about the magic that happens when new meets old," says Cullman. "The new has to learn from the old, and the old has to learn from the new. That mix makes interiors so much more vibrant and interesting."

LEFT: Andrew Allfree pairs casually draped velvet and bold hues at Château de Montigny-sur-Avre in Normandy, France.

OPPOSITE: Gold frames pop against the board-and-batten walls of John Oetgen's North Carolina getaway house.

Occasional Chairs

It's rare for a designer to intentionally seek out an uncomfortable piece of furniture, but it's a rule they might break for the "occasional chair," a seldom-used piece that's commonly cast aside and then rescued from an antiques store. These dramatic little seats can offer an arresting sculptural display—where graphic slabs of exposed wood grain can become a moment of haute art. In falling-apart red velvet and time-worn wood, they evoke another era and bring a sense of history to a modern space, whether fireside in a living room, adjacent to a soaking tub in the master bath, or lining a hallway. And while you wouldn't want to perch on one for very long, they can happily support a stack of coffee table books even better than the coffee table itself—which may find more fitting use holding your cappuccino.

ABOVE: Pale walls set off the mix of antiquities and antiques—such as a Roman marble corbel—in John Saladino's Montecito, California, residence.

OPPOSITE: Sculptural furniture sets a playful tone in Stephen Sills's living room, which opens to the lush outdoors of Bedford, New York.

ABOVE: A lush piece of art by Carol Greenan Bouyoucos lends this Upper East Side sitting area designed by Ashley Whittaker an alfresco air.

RIGHT: A 17th-century Italian console stands out in Antony Todd's pared-down Manhattan space.

OPPOSITE: Architect D. Stanley Dixon was inspired by rural English architecture in this Atlanta home; decorator Carolyn Malone selected window treatments to match the linen-hued walls for a calming look.

"My propensity–particularly in a modern vernacular– is a need for an antique or primitive piece to lend interest to environments that otherwise feel formulaic. So many interiors these days feel so much the same. George III side tables tend to be very pure; Louis XVI chairs are a more elaborate foil."

DARRYL CARTER, DESIGNER

PAGES 24-25: Dress a room in layers for a cozy vibe, as in this Palm Beach living room designed by Bunny Williams. "When you do one color, it's less busy," she says.

OPPOSITE: Firewood becomes an art piece in designer Darryl Carter's Washington, D.C., garden room, where a reclaimed 19th-century barn door hides a TV.

Dotting a room with finds from your travels will call to mind your favorite memories on life's inevitable drizzly days.

OPPOSITE: Design historian Maureen Footer installed objects from her travels, such as a Sultanabad rug, in her Manhattan library. "These finds remind me of where I've been and what I've discovered along the way."

PAGES 28-29: High-gloss walls turn this Richard Keith Langham–designed Pennsylvania room into a jewel box.

ABOVE LEFT: Display your most loved treasures so they bring you joy constantly, such as this custom hat from New York milliner Suzanne Newman atop an 18th-century bust in Maureen Footer's Manhattan abode.

ABOVE RIGHT: Custom leather shelf edging on a bookcase supplies a touch of personalized glamour in design historian Maureen Footer's Manhattan apartment.

LIVING ROOMS 31

ABOVE: Cream paneled walls make this large Quogue, New York, family room designed by Amanda Nisbet feel more intimate.

RIGHT: A 19th-century marble-top table divides a double living room in Provence—designed by Bunny Williams—into two sitting areas. The designer famously scours local markets and shops for one-of-a-kind items. "Every room gets triggered by something—often, a great discovery," she says.

ABOVE: A vintage bird print establishes the blue-and-white scheme in a Windsor, Florida, suite by Alessandra Branca. "I wanted a neutral palette," Branca says. "This is beachy and loose."

PAGE 34: In a Palm Beach living room designed by Susan Zises Green, a palette of pinks, creams, and corals echoes a collection of seashells.

PAGE 35: Sheathed in silver leaf and finished in golden Venetian wax, a Manhattan living room ceiling designed by Alecia Stevens and architect Nate McBride shimmers at night.

ABOVE: Tiny touches—such as a fringed skirt on the sofa and scrolled arms on a pair of chairs—provide a careful, studied appearance in this Palm Beach home.

RIGHT: A French gilt mirror hangs above an antique pearwood chest in this Atlanta living room designed by Carolyn Malone.

PAGES 36-37: Walls paneled in southern cypress echo the beach outside in this home designed by Thomas A. Kligerman, with interior design by Mia Jung. Kligerman calls this East Coast project his "experiment with a traditional New England house. The big question was, how modern can I make it without losing the character that makes it so special?"

ABOVE: Painting a rounded ceiling in high-gloss lacquer shows off its curves in this Hamptons, Long Island, home designed by Amanda Nisbet.

LEFT: Fermoire cotton turns a window seat cushion in a Connecticut home designed by Timothy Whealon into a place for lingering with a delicious book.

LIVING ROOMS 39

Smart Public Art

A living room necessitates a few conversation pieces, and little gets you and your guests from greeting to tête-à-tête faster than evocative and absorbing art. Consider a pair of ombré paintings that draws the eye to nowhere and the mind to everywhere; or a verdant oversize landscape photograph that brings the feeling of a garden walk to any urban environment. Consider an antique tapestry that conjures old Europe; or a staid oil portrait of an imagined ancestor whose watchful eyes will remind you to limit your screen time, because life is short. Whatever you decorate with, select beautiful pieces that have special meaning for you. Every time you contemplate it, you'll likely find new meaning within it—and new, inspiring appreciation within yourself.

ABOVE: A 19th-century tapestry becomes unforgettable art hung above the fireplace mantel in a Montecito, California, room designed by Ann Holden. "The look is traditional but current," Holden says. "It's a balance."

OPPOSITE: A stately Newport study is brought to life by a jazzy tiger print and orange curtains by Ruthie Sommers.

ABOVE: Designer Betsy Brown added texture and warmth to minimalist rooms in Charlotte, North Carolina, and separated them with flowing creamy draperies. "You position unlike pieces close together, but with air around them so they show up, spark each other, and come alive," Brown says. "That contrast is what gives the room a kinetic quality and makes it feel interesting."

PAGES 42-43: A photograph with great depth of field expands the sitting area in a Windsor, Florida, room by Alessandra Branca.

LEFT: Candles and greenery in an 18th-century Wedgwood pot sit atop a painted chest in Suzanne Rheinstein's Louisiana-inspired Los Angeles library. "Candles make everything look great, including guests," she says.

OPPOSITE: Artist Kate Cordsen imbued the living room of her Italianate Victorian, which is set on a bluff overlooking the Connecticut River, with Victorian grandeur and Japanese-inspired restraint.

"The most important thing for me is that people see the relevance of antiques, including 18th-century furniture. Why do we make so much new stuff when we've got such beautiful old things? Of course I use quality new pieces too, but I mix it up. Antiques just need to be used in the right way."

ALEX PAPACHRISTIDIS, DESIGNER

OPPOSITE: Couture dressmaker touches give this Manhattan sitting room by Alex Papachristidis polish and pizzazz.

ABOVE: Purple accents cozy up Colette van den Thillart's Toronto sitting room, awash in warm neutrals. She made the plaster piece above the settee. "When I need something with personality, I sometimes just make it myself," she says.

RIGHT: Venetian-plaster walls give an eclectic Upper East Side living room designed by Ashley Whittaker a serene backdrop.

ABOVE: Large-print gingham window treatments add necessary playfulness to this Palm Beach living room.

LEFT: A pair of ombré paintings by Pieter Vermeersch add subtle depth to a Hamptons living room designed by Luis Bustamante with architecture by Steven Harris. "You don't ever want to get stuck," says the client of her art collection. "There are always new things to learn and a world that is unfolding."

Exquisite details make for exquisite moments. Embroidered paneling and tiny antique prints delight both the eye and mind.

OPPOSITE: A Florian Schulz pendant balances a 1940s Danish desk in a New York City library designed by Tammy Connor.

ABOVE LEFT: In an 1850 Lancaster County, Pennsylvania, farmhouse designed by Richard Keith Langham, a circa-1900 crewel panel hangs in a gilt frame. The Georgian armchair is from the estate of silent film star Mary Pickford.

ABOVE RIGHT: Antique oak paneling gives architect James Carter's Birmingham, Alabama, library a warm, weathered look.

Classical Listening

One of the easiest ways to bring beauty into your life today was once much rarer than gold: classical music and opera. Such audible delights weren't commonly enjoyed by the masses until the late 19th century, with the advent of Thomas Edison's phonograph, and the fact that most of us now walk around with limitless songs on our phones would shock and delight Wolfgang Amadeus Mozart and his ilk. More than a thrill for the ears, these harmonics are a balm for the soul, bringing an art form once enjoyed by royal courts into every country cabin and urban pied-à-terre. If you're feeling listless, plug Lakmé's Flower Duet into Spotify, settle into a particularly cozy nook in your living room, close your eyes, and really listen. You'll feel reborn.

ABOVE: Cuttings from a Japanese maple tree exude wild glamour in Michael DePerno and Andrew Fry's third-floor design studio in Litchfield County, Connecticut.

OPPOSITE: Pearl and caramel hues are punctuated by exultant sapphire textiles in this New York City Upper East Side sitting area by Nick Olsen.

ABOVE: Consider breaking up an open-plan living space with screens for a sense of intimacy, such as in Bobby McAlpine's Atlanta sitting area of stark-white furniture silhouetted against wood-paneled walls.

RIGHT: A bar cabinet in Thomas O'Brien and Dan Fink's Bellport, New York, library shows off vintage Steuben, Baccarat, and Heisey glassware.

OPPOSITE: A framed 18th-century Japanese textile and colorful patterned pillows brighten the Lipari, Italy, off-white living room of Nicola and Elda Fabrizio, cofounders of Dedar fabrics.

ABOVE: Elegant architecture and a muted palette designed by Tammy Connor keep the focus on this New York City living room's breathtaking views of Central Park. "The interiors must speak to the setting, or we're not doing our job," Connor says.

PAGES 56-57: Bronze window casings frame floor-to-ceiling mountain views in this Aspen getaway designed by Victoria Hagan, with architecture by Joeb Moore.

RIGHT: Separate seating areas make a large salon designed by Madeline Stuart feel intimate and furry rugs underfoot provide instant coziness.

ABOVE: If dazzling hues make you happy, don't hold back. Tiger velvet, spring color, and far-flung artifacts reinterpret Dior's decorating in Maureen Footer's Manhattan living room.

LEFT: Creamy white sheer curtains create a sense of calm in a living room in Israel by Houston designer Kevin Spearman.

CHAPTER TWO

Sunrooms

If you're lucky enough to have a sunroom in your home, then you're very lucky indeed.

They conjure the salad days of summer in their very name: not rain, not sleet, not fog, not hurricane, but transcendent sun, the orb that has the power to transform our outlook after just a few moments of basking in its glow. Also called the solarium—Latin for "place of sunlight"—is it any wonder that these spaces, where sunlight flows in like warm honey, are among the most delightful rooms to decorate? They can be lined in buttoned-up trelliage, evocative of the manicured gardens of Versailles, for a classicist's élan, or given a sky-blue ceiling as dreamy as a cloudless July afternoon. Dotting the walls with 18th-century botanical drawings brings the lushness of the garden indoors year-round. However you approach their design, bring in happy touches and it will convey the spirit of a sun-soaked day—no matter the forecast.

PAGES 60-61: Bronze railings and diaphanous curtains in John Oetgen's mountain retreat transform a screened porch into a refined outdoor salon. "I wanted something that matches the lifestyle here: people in khaki shorts and boots piling in from a hike for a big meal, and dogs running around everywhere," Oetgen says.

OPPOSITE: The walls can make the room. Here, a soothing, trellis-clad sunroom in Dallas designed by Cathy Kincaid.

ABOVE: In this Alabama sunroom, Mark D. Sikes framed a garden view with drapery in the same leafy print he used on the wicker chair cushions. "It's as if this house says 'hello' when you walk in—it tells you a story, then it sings to you," Sikes says. "And when you leave, you feel loved."

RIGHT: Inspired by archival botanical prints from the 18th century, decoupage artist John Derian makes time to slow down and paint. "I love the idea of re-sharing lessons from another time," he says.

OPPOSITE: A sunporch on Michael DePerno and Andrew Fry's Connecticut property becomes a summertime dream room with a vintage wrought-iron table and antique painted chairs. "We work very much in the old-fashioned style," DePerno explains.

SUNROOMS 65

Homey Houseplants

In the 19th century, when Samuel Clemens (better known as Mark Twain) and his architects designed his family's Gothic Revival home in Hartford, Connecticut, he was careful to include one very important thing: a conservatory. The lush, plant-stocked room became a junglelike reprieve from his stresses—and his three daughters loved it so much they cheekily nicknamed the space The Jungle. Those Victorians were on to something. Brought indoors, live plants can be nearly as restorative as a garden walk, adding verdant grace to any surface or empty corner. Try an orangery stocked with Nagami kumquat trees or tabletop potted succulents that require so little, yet give so much. There's nothing that brings more life to a room, literally.

ABOVE: Architect Alexandre Lafourcade designed an airy orangery in a Provence home for the owner's Nagami kumquat trees. The flooring is limestone and the windows are framed in iron.

OPPOSITE: A maidenhair fern and topiary add a note of classicism to this bold, blue room designed by Nick Olsen.

"**The magic of a sunroom is that sense that you are almost outside—that you are sheltered in a delicate, almost fragile way from the elements, whether the sun or a drizzling rain.**"

THOMAS A. KLIGERMAN, ARCHITECT

PAGES 68-69: A sky-blue ceiling lends an ethereal note to an orangery in Dallas designed by Cathy Kincaid with architecture by J. Wilson Fuqua. "It's a dreamy place for luncheons or cocktails before dinner," Kincaid says.

OPPOSITE: Various textures—linen, rattan, teak—combine for earthy beauty in this New England sunporch by architect Thomas A. Kligerman.

OPPOSITE: Turquoise steel-cased windows evoke Old Hollywood, Art Deco allure in this Hollywood sunroom with interiors by Madeline Stuart and architectural renovation by Kevin A. Clark.

ABOVE: White upholstery glows in the light of a Charlotte, North Carolina, sunroom by Betsy Brown. "When you use a lot of neutrals, it's really about the contrast in forms and textures," Brown says. "That's what gives a room a kinetic quality."

Woven Wonders

We have the ancient Egyptians to thank for pioneering a host of life's simpler pleasures—from feline adoration and sundials to paper. No surprise that these sun worshippers invented something integral to today's solariums: wicker furniture (Tutankhamen himself was buried with a wicker chair made of entwined reeds). It's just as beloved today for adding laid-back, earthy texture to a room, whether it's hewn of cane, rattan, willow, or bamboo. In a seaside estate or San Francisco pied-à-terre, it says "summah" year-round.

ABOVE: Inlaid seashells embellish the loggia's French doors in this 1920s Palm Beach retreat designed by the homeowner.

OPPOSITE: Artist Kate Cordsen's New England porch serves as a welcoming outdoor living room and nook for alfresco entertaining, complete with a 19th-century wicker bar cart.

OPPOSITE: A loggia in this 1920s Palm Beach home designed by Susan Zises Green extends outside the living room, with detailed painted ceilings that draw the eye up and out to the serene skies beyond. "My goal was to lighten and brighten and create a joyous environment in which to live," the designer says.

ABOVE: Geometric tile lends a modern edge to a Dallas sunroom designed by Cathy Kincaid. "The colors and patterns talk to each other rather than collide," the designer says. "The more you add, the less busy it can seem."

CHAPTER THREE

Gardens

The ancient Roman philosopher Marcus Tullius Cicero said it best: "If you have a garden and a library, you have everything you need."

Long before technology began to muddle our days, he knew that leafy plots had the power to elevate the senses, awakening a primal satisfaction that recalls the garden of Eden—for where there are plants, there is water, the fount of all life. To make your garden as gorgeous as can be, whether it's the size of the manicured grounds of Château de Villandry in the Loire Valley or a more modest setting, keep symmetry top of mind. You could, for example, turn Japanese boxwood hedges into a moment of artful sculpture. Or fashion an allée—a row of plantings on either side of your entrance evocative of Louisiana's Oak Alley Plantation—of hornbeam hedges, lamb's ears, and plane trees for the most evocative welcome home possible. Another approach: Erect an arched arbor, plant some David Austin climbing roses, and do what Mother Nature intends: Let them roam wild. The more they cavort across the structure, the more they satisfy our souls.

PAGES 78-79: Japanese boxwood hedges fashion a sculptural, formal approach to the brick Tudor-style Memphis home of designer and antiques dealer William Eubanks, which is cloaked with ivy, white O'Hara roses, and creeping fig. "I don't think there's ever a bad view out of my window," he says.

OPPOSITE: Cypress trees evoke the south of France at this Los Angeles estate with landscape architecture by Perry Guillot.

ABOVE: Boxwood can lend a whiff of the classic, especially when planted in pots and used in multiples. Here, a modern arrangement at a contemporary Atlanta home.

LEFT: Make a statement by installing one large urn as an art piece in a garden corner, such as this one in a Santa Barbara, California, home designed by Ann Holden.

OPPOSITE: A peacock named Brunelleschi struts the 17th-century formal gardens of designer Juan Pablo Molyneux's estate south of Paris.

"Gardens should reveal themselves slowly. That's why creating spots for intimate moments and unexpected places to gather is so important. With seating, lighting, and a source of warmth, a secret garden can become another environment for living and entertaining."

SCOTT SHRADER, LANDSCAPE DESIGNER

OPPOSITE: A lotus pond and gurgling fountains turn Richard Hallberg's Montecito home into an escape. "If I'm here, I'm on vacation," he says. "It's like I've left the States."

Pristine Plantings

Most of us have resigned ourselves to the fact that we will never live in an actual castle. And yet the gardens of most are attainable for all, albeit in a smaller footprint. You may not have the yardage, but a plant is a plant—an achievable purchase no matter the size of your domain. When you're exploring some of the world's grandest gardens, there are a few types of princely flora you'll spy again and again (often planted in gardens with a limited color palette, be it all white or all mauve). Take boxwood, which conjures the 9,500-hundred-acre topiary garden of England's Levens Hall and is every bit as lushly lovely (yet requires only an annual or biannual trimming to retain its regal shape). Olive trees will transport you to the sun-dappled groves of Salento, Italy, in an instant. Same goes for towering cypress trees—they're as much at home in California as they are on the hillocks of the south of France.

ABOVE: To make a statement, go big with your flora—as with these agave salmiana and olive trees in a Malibu courtyard garden by Scott Shrader.

OPPOSITE: White daybeds draw the eye to the turquoise pool on this terrace on the Caribbean island of Mustique designed by Veere Grenney.

GARDENS

ABOVE: An outdoor fireplace nestled under the eaves of a Malibu courtyard by Scott Shrader creates a primal lure.

RIGHT: Verdant and versatile topiaries' carefully clipped shrubs displayed en masse will put a little spring in any space.

PAGES 88-89: Adding formal structure to Oprah Winfrey's Montecito cutting garden: myrtle topiaries and border bushes of Honey Dijon and Tuscan Sun roses.

ABOVE: A flowing tablecloth evokes romance in an alfresco dining room, such as this Malibu courtyard by landscape designer Scott Shrader.

LEFT: Functional moments can be exquisite, such as this built-in Malibu potting area by Scott Shrader.

Symmetry is one secret to enduring style—there's little more that's timeless, especially when you add lush, leafy greenery in abundance.

ABOVE LEFT: Potted begonias and a fig tree flank the entrance to a walled garden in the Bellport, Long Island, getaway of Thomas O'Brien and Dan Fink.

ABOVE RIGHT: The sound of bubbling water is inherently soothing and ideal for an entrance courtyard; this fountain, in a Malibu garden by landscape architect Scott Shrader, was hewn from a reclaimed wellhead.

OPPOSITE: A covered bench in Colette van den Thillart's Canadian garden provides shady respite on warm days.

Architecture Alfresco

Opposites attract. In the sartorial world, that often equates to pairing a flouncy blouse with sleek black pants. But in the garden, it means you can maximize the unkempt, boundless beauty of nature by giving it something stolid and unyielding and architectural with which to contrast. Traditional built-in seating can offset all the resplendent wild growth adjacent; a bougainvillea-swathed pergola draws the eye to another level, much like a butterfly flitting skyward.

ABOVE: Architectural structures, such as this trellis with bougainvillea designed for a Malibu home by Scott Shrader, help break up expansive gardens.

OPPOSITE: Piped upholstery adds a classic vibe amid the wildness of designer and antiques dealer William Eubanks's Memphis garden.

ABOVE: Overhead lanterns on the arbor of this Bunny Williams–designed home in the south of France allow for dinner parties into the wee hours. Gardens are central to the Provençal lifestyle, and this one, by Tim Rees, "is especially magical," Williams says. The family spends sun-soaked afternoons under the shade of the arbor while the unofficial mascot of the region, the cicada, chirps overhead.

PAGES 96-97: A neutral palette reigns in Bobby McAlpine's Atlanta garden, which is framed by a gusty arrangement of lush green boxwoods and other well-tended plants. True color, McAlpine says, comes from "living things—our beloved friends, cherished animals, and well-tended plants."

LEFT: With a multicolored candelabra, mismatched chairs, and pink linen-topped table, Kathryn M. Ireland's Provençal farm becomes the ultimate place for a bucolic bite.

OPPOSITE: Event designer Keith Robinson serves blackberry hand pies with fresh blackberry jam on his Georgia estate—as if to say there is no such thing as too much.

Outdoor Living

The wisest landscape designers think like interior designers—at least when arranging alfresco seating areas. They are, after all, our living rooms unbound and should be treated as such. Just as everyone needs a comfortable seat and a place to set their cocktail in the living room, the same is required en plein air. Creature comforts become even more pivotal beyond the confines of architecture, when more than the slightest of breezes can have a jarring effect. Cozy up your outdoor dining area with plush seats you can sink into, and fashion a built-in sofa that will stand up to all seasons. Invest in a space heater or, at the very least, a hidden trove of throw blankets you can pull out as dusk descends. Who wants the arriving chill to force them back inside just as the sky is turning a tawny pink and lavender? Not us.

ABOVE: Create a cozy perch to pamper both yourself and four-legged friends, such as this Malibu built-in sofa near raised herb and vegetable beds by landscape architect Scott Shrader. "The grounds provide endless opportunities for entertaining," Shrader says. "I love the intimacy and scale of it. It feels like someone wrapping their arms around you."

OPPOSITE: Placing comfortable seating around an Italian stone table encourages guests to linger on this Tel Aviv garden terrace with design by Kevin Spearman and a landscape by Jean Mus.

"Sometimes I stand under the arbor, close my eyes, and allow myself to take in as much as I can: I hear birds splashing in the fountain and literally smell the roses. This garden makes me present."

OPRAH WINFREY ON HER MONTECITO, CALIFORNIA, HOME

OPPOSITE: In Oprah's 65-acre Montecito, California garden, Tuscan Sun, Honey Dijon, Seafoam and Fragrant Cloud roses are underplanted with dahlias, lilies, narcissi, daffodils, irises, and blooming annuals and perennials to provide color all year long.

One reason to ensure your outdoor areas are as delightful as your rooms: They maximize your living space. And who doesn't want to toast to cocktail hour alfresco?

OPPOSITE: Elegant table settings dress up sunset dinners on the dock at designer Colette van den Thillart's Canadian lake house.

ABOVE LEFT: A table overlooking the garden is set with platters of cheese and citrus in the Los Angeles home of designer Suzanne Rheinstein.

ABOVE RIGHT: The table is set for entertaining under an arbor of blooming Lady Banks roses on Keith Robinson's Georgia plantation.

ABOVE: With overflowing lavender beds, outdoor spaces blend seamlessly with interiors in Steve and Brooke Giannetti's Ojai, California, home.

RIGHT: A series of arbors covered with roses evoke Claude Monet's gardens at Giverny.

OPPOSITE: Bamboo structures in Connecticut vegetable gardens designed by Deborah Nevins allow climbing vines to flourish and provide graphic splendor.

PAGE 108: Don't forget to look up. Here, a loggia beckons in a historic 1928 Palm Beach house built by architect Maurice Fatio and redecorated by Susan Zises Green.

PAGE 109: Add a sense of history to new builds, such as the West Palm Beach home of designer Lars Bolander. The garden-facing facade features an oval plaque that once adorned a California winery, along with a pair of 100-year-old Brazilian doors. "Lars may be Swedish by birth," his wife, Parisian artist Nadine Kalachnikoff, says, "but he's not very Swedish in his mind." Swedes, she explains, tend to be practical; they like things for their function. Her husband, she notes, will often opt for "beauty for beauty's sake."

CHAPTER FOUR

Dining Rooms

If kitchens are the heart of the home, dining rooms are the stage—a theatrical locale where your guests

will soak up an evening dinner party, talking and laughing well into the night. So do as the 20th-century famed socialite Marie-Hélène de Rothschild would do and put on a show, not only for them, but for yourself. Dining rooms, like your best china, are meant to be used, so make them pretty. This is the place to invest in touches with cinematic chops—intricate custom plasterwork inspired by Morocco for the walls, perhaps, or hand-painted wallpaper, such as Gracie's chinoiserie panels, made since 1898—that seem like haute art (or at least something storied, even if you're in a newly built manse). Some designers go the other direction, matching drapery and upholstered walls to create a jewel box. If nothing else, cushy seats are a must—at least, if you want your guests to linger and love it.

PAGES 110-111: Restrict your color palette—it won't feel like a restriction if they're your favorite hues. In this Palm Beach dining room by designer Phoebe Howard, stripes and florals mix with ease in preppy blue and white. "The client was craving sun, light, and fresh air," the designer says. "She told me, 'I want the colors you see in Palm Beach: the flora, the sea, the sky.' "

OPPOSITE: Allow greens to delight in unlikely places. This Mark D. Sikes-designed Alabama dining room's garden view is always in bloom with hand-painted wallcovering by Gracie.

ABOVE: A Palm Beach dining room is enveloped in a Venetian plaster in a custom shade that its designer, Susan Zises Green, calls "lettuce green." "My goal," the designer says, "is to create a joyous environment in which to live."

RIGHT: As Luther Burbank, American botanist and horticulturalist, said, "Flowers always make people better, happier, and more hopeful; they are sunshine, food, and medicine to the soul."

ABOVE: A gilded iron lantern gives an old country-inspired Atlanta dining room designed by Carolyn Malone with architecture by D. Stanley Dixon a genial glow.

LEFT: Sprinkling amethyst accents throughout this formal Atlanta dining room by Melanie Turner gives it a fresh verve. The house "was just this big, vanilla box," Turner says. "So we layered in a lot of details."

ABOVE: In a Palm Beach villa with interior design by the homeowner, a mirrored cabinet glitters amid the dining room's soft, pale hues (note the monogrammed dining chairs).

OPPOSITE: Slipcovers and a breezy print tablecloth offset the formal touches in this Palm Beach dining room.

"Nothing is more important in a dining room than bringing focus to the center of the table. Spectacular light fixtures that create beautiful light levels are the key in creating a dynamic and flattering focus for all at the table."

THOMAS PHEASANT, DESIGNER

OPPOSITE: An adventurous color, citron, feels harmonious in this Washington, D.C., dining room designed by Thomas Pheasant with draperies matched to the walls in a Romo fabric. Before long, that warm, inviting glow made the room a favorite gathering place.

ABOVE: Five coats of Limoges Blue paint applied with a strié technique achieve a lustrous hue in the dining room of this Virginia home designed by Suzanne Kasler. "So much of the success of the interior lay in how we treated color," Kasler says.

RIGHT: A Fairfield County, Connecticut, butler's pantry designed by Timothy Whealon transforms into the perfect cutting room for blooms from the garden.

PAGES 120-121: Any find can be retrofitted to suit your lifestyle—such as these antique lanterns constructed of vintage parts purchased in France and hung on custom trapezes in Bobby McAlpine's Atlanta salon.

OPPOSITE: A custom wicker table and chairs thoroughly evoke their Caribbean Mustique home in this dining room by Veere Grenney.

Top Tablescapes

Aesthetes well know that what you place on a table is just as important as what you place on a plate, and texture is vital for an elegant scene. Twinkling candles are the quickest way to cast a fairy-tale glow over your guests, but they're just one of countless ways to set a delightful mood. Copious amounts of fresh-cut roses will turn any tabletop into a riotous flower bed. Feathers, when corralled in simple silver vases, have the same softening effect as bouquets of peonies and can be used year-round. Whatever you decide, be sure to arrange centerpieces and select plates, silverware, and stemware that will captivate and charm your guests. Make the evening's menu harmonize with the decor by turning the dishes into art itself—for example, by topping a simple salad with nasturtium blossoms—and the memory of it will be just as beautiful as it was delicious.

ABOVE: Dotting a tablescape with fresh-cut blooms makes guests feel as if they've stepped foot into a secret garden, such as this textured New York table by decoupage by artist John Derian.

OPPOSITE: The hand-painted wallpaper's architectural elements are echoed in the crown molding's honeycomb pattern in this Manhattan room by Alex Papachristidis.

OPPOSITE: Use mirrors to reflect your most treasured objects, such as in this Palm Beach dining room designed by Bunny Williams.

ABOVE: Designer Antony Todd sets his Manhattan apartment's custom-made white oak table with vermeil chargers and feather-stuffed tumblers as eye candy. It adds to the intimacy of his dinner parties: "I learned from my godmother: She would politely insist that everyone actually listen to everyone else, instead of just talking over each other. She really encouraged her guests to share and connect."

DINING ROOMS 127

PAGES 128-129: A collection of antique Delftware and faience pottery crowns a gilt-wood mirror in this Provence dining room by Susan Bednar Long.

ABOVE: Luminous details such as lacquer, gilt, and bronze help transform this Park Avenue dining room, with interior design and architecture by Thomas Pheasant, into a theater in the round. Curved cabinet doors and a plaster corona overhead spin the illusion of a grand rotunda. Rather than raise the curtain on one big reveal, Pheasant prefers staging revelations that gradually emerge over time through a scrim of simplicity. Case in point: "The clients called after a dinner party to say how excited they were. They'd never noticed until then the way my Willow chandelier casts a leafy canopy overhead at night."

ABOVE: Ethereal custom walls are topped with a delicate hand-painted ceiling mural in John Saladino's dining room, nestled in the picturesque hills of Santa Barbara County, California.

LEFT: Opt for extremely touchable fabrics. In this Provence dining room designed by Susan Bednar Long, damaske Braquenié draperies lined in a Chelsea Editions check flank a bust statue.

"Choose a color scheme and be true to it…if it is blue and white, treat it as a monochromatic scheme. Use it everywhere, and then throw in another color as the accent."

ALESSANDRA BRANCA, DESIGNER

OPPOSITE: Unexpected china and flatware puts a smile on guests' faces, such as in this sunny seat in a Windsor, Florida, getaway designed by Alessandra Branca.

ABOVE: The centerpiece of Keith Robinson's Georgia table includes Campanella roses, peaches-and-cream dahlias, and camellia and artemisia foliage.

OPPOSITE: Designer Juan Pablo Molyneaux commissioned a fanciful motif of hot-air balloons by artist Frédéric Monpoint on the original paneling of the tower of his chateau, set 30 miles south of Paris in Pouy-sur-Vannes.

PAGES 136-137: A striped sofa sets a restrained tone in the dining room of Michael DePerno and Andrew Fry's Connecticut home, with its American Empire table and antique English Chippendale chairs.

The Light Fantastic

If you've ever settled in for an evening at the Metropolitan Opera in Manhattan, you likely remember one thing more than the aria and even the sets. You remember the lighting. Designed in 1966 by Austrian Hans Harald Rath, the Swarovski crystal starburst chandeliers rise along with the curtain like a meteor shower over a starless city. Your dining room deserves the same treatment. What could you install that would put the fab in fabulous? A glimmering antique French chandelier hung low over an oval table, or a pair of Sputnik-inspired pendant lights that cast the entire party in a come-hither glow. Be sure to add a dimmer—you'll want to soften the lighting to set an instant mood.

ABOVE: Playful colors lend a carefree air to the formal dining room designed by Ruthie Sommers.

OPPOSITE: Amanda Lindroth's seagrass pitcher and glasses summon her Palm Beach locale.

We have nothing against plain walls (or plain china, for that matter). But sometimes, a little adornment makes your dining experience that much more delectable.

OPPOSITE: The dining room of this Dallas home designed by Emily Summers with architecture by Marc Appleton is filled with hand-crafted details inspired by Morocco.

ABOVE LEFT: Custom plasterwork in a Dallas dining room designed by Emily Summers evokes a Moroccan motif.

ABOVE RIGHT: Show off a collection, like pottery vessels, with various flower varieties in a limited palette.

ABOVE: Touches of red infuse a neutral dining room in a Hamptons, Long Island, weekend home designed with warmth by Luis Bustamante.

LEFT: Cotton slipcovers and an abaca rug take this Connecticut dining room's formality down a notch. Designer Timothy Whealon was going for a "modern farmhouse feel—elegant but not too fussy."

OPPOSITE: Draping linens softens the beamed ceiling in this Connecticut dining room designed by Brooke and Steve Giannetti.

DINING ROOMS 143

ABOVE: Marble plinths support a bounty of satsumas and French cheese placed atop the custom concrete, steel, and plexiglass dining table in Darryl Carter's Beaux Arts Washington, D.C., townhouse.

OPPOSITE: Combining disparate design epochs creates a timeless effect. Modern furniture contrasts with a traditional backdrop—an Aubusson tapestry—in author Maureen Footer's Manhattan dining room.

CHAPTER FIVE

Kitchens

When you hear the words Director Nancy Meyers, what comes to mind? Diane Keaton and rom-coms, to be sure.

But you likely also conjure kitchens. Meyers has made a name for herself that transcends cinema by setting key scenes in the home's most primally satisfying room. Her cookspaces are gleaming, pristine, and inviting. They're memorable because they're more than functional—they're warm in a way that epitomizes "home." To get a similar effect, opt for one uniform color—such as a powder-blue gray—for cabinets paired with handsome brass hardware for a sense of history. Even hanging a collection of gleaming copper pots says, "I'm the next Julia Child," whether or not you mean it. Or take it in an entirely different cinematic direction—to a French castle via Ojai, California—with white-oak cabinetry in honeyed tones and a limestone backsplash, lavender bursting on the countertop.

PAGES 146-147: Walls in Breccia Imperiale marble create textural interest in an open-plan Westchester County, New York, kitchen by Jim Howard. The designer believes he has done his job effectively when nothing in particular stands out. "My goal is to design an overall experience—something so balanced that it isn't about just one thing," he says.

OPPOSITE: Leather barstools, a limestone hood, and Italian Paonazzo marble counters lend storied heft to this Southern California kitchen designed by Laurie Steichen with architecture by M. Carbine Restorations. A stack of antique tiles was repurposed as a new floor, and an 18th-century painted cabinet purchased at a Paris flea market became a marble-topped island.

ABOVE: Mark D. Sikes kept the original happy cabinet lining in this Alabama home to bring his clients joy, day after day. "The home teems with little decorative flourishes—wallpapered ceilings, painted millwork—that other clients might have shied away from," the designer says.

ABOVE: English and Continental creamware create an eye-catching pattern around John Saladino's round kitchen window in his Montecito, California, home. The designer recently downsized. "I brought only my most treasured things," he says. His chosen belongings are emblematic of his seminal style, and each one ignites joy.

LEFT: "I love kitchens," says designer Stephen Sills, "but it's very contradictory, because I normally don't like anything utilitarian." In his space in Bedford, New York, he has married form and function with aplomb: raw-cypress islands were inspired by worktables in historic English estates, while crisp quartz countertops and stainless steel cabinets are set against French limestone floors.

Divine Backsplashes

Even the humblest, most utilitarian stove can stand to play dress-up. Figuratively speaking, that means one thing: a showstopping backsplash. Because these often take the form of nearly permanent art, select something you'll never tire of. Some kitchen designers are opting for the classic and pristine look of white marble slabs, which, matched to the counter, create the seamless and seraphic effect of a Grecian emple. Others prefer to charm à la Portugal's azulejo tiles, creating a full wall of blue-and-white tile grid that summons the Palace of the Marquesses of Fronteira in Lisbon at a glance.

ABOVE: This Aspen kitchen designed by J. Randall Powers was modeled on European country homes, with pendant lights over the island to highlight the sky-high exposed-beam ceilings.

OPPOSITE: A sweet tile backsplash counteracts a sleek industrial lacquered island in this Windsor, Florida, cookspace designed by Alessandra Branca.

ABOVE: Brass details elevate an all-white kitchen in Atlanta's leafy Buckhead district by designer Melanie Turner.

LEFT: Oak interior drawers complement matte stainless steel cabinetry in Stephen Sills's kitchen. "Cooking, for me, is a creative outlet," he says—so he has equipped himself with every requisite accoutrement.

OPPOSITE: A white-on-white-on-white kitchen puts the focus on the food in Nicola and Elda Fabrizio's Italian home. "We wanted the interior to be very simple and light-filled, with just a touch of color," says Elda. Whitewashed inside and out, the home gives the impression that the Fabrizios have lived in it for decades.

KITCHENS 155

"I love to collect mementos from my travels around the world and bring them home to remind me of where I have been. Whatever your passion is, it's fun and rewarding to collect treasures over the years. Like items grouped together is beautiful, makes an impact, and tells a story about what you love."

MARK D. SIKES, DESIGNER

OPPOSITE: By lacquering the bar of this Hamptons, Long Island, home in deep navy blue, Amanda Nisbet allowed the shellcraft lantern to pop. "It's important to acknowledge where you are—in this case, a beach house—but that doesn't mean giving in to tired notions," she says.

Counter Culture

Kitchen designers can argue into the wee hours on the merits of butler sinks and under-counter refrigerator drawers, but there's one thing in particular they lose sleep over: countertops. The array of options is downright dizzying, each with sundry perks and pitfalls. Italian marble nods to epochal European cathedrals but can bring a grown man to tears after a Cabernet spill. Tech-forward options, such as Glassos from CCS Stone, can appear as polished as a Middleton. Opt for whichever finish will make you merry when you're bleary-eyed and awaiting caffeine, and you'll never regret it.

ABOVE: A soothing atmosphere requires simplicity and order—such as in this Aspen kitchen designed by Victoria Hagan with architect Joeb Moore. "I love the juxtaposition of the organic geometry with the rugged wildness of the outdoors," Hagan says.

OPPOSITE: Graphic backsplash tiles ground the room in this Los Angeles estate designed in Louis XV style by Anthony Baratta, with architecture by Steve Giannetti. Baratta's clients, who delight in giving parties and epicurean dinners, "don't just love to entertain," he says, laughing. "They're the ultimate hosts."

CHAPTER SIX

Breakfast Rooms

Though nutrition science leaves room for debate, anyone who has ever slogged through a morning meeting while "hangry" knows the truth:

Breakfast is unquestionably the most important meal of the day. So why not start it right by creating a space that's the poetic equivalent of sun streaming down on a tray of warm croissants and fresh-squeezed orange juice? In a breakfast room, happiness reigns. Because these spaces often have a small footprint, it's the ideal place to go big and bold. You could, for example, line the entire wall from floor to ceiling with plate rails—and the requisite gilt china—to start each day with a feeling of tidy bounty. Or place a citrus tree—kaffir lime, Meyer lemon, and the like—in every corner for a stimulating scent that nods to the orangeries of the Jardin des Tuileries. Opt for bliss in every decorating decision, and it will be the best part of waking up.

PAGES 160-161: In a Provence room designed by Bunny Williams, an antique French tole chandelier hangs over this breakfast table covered in a tablecloth in a Provencal style fabric. Portuguese tile create a mural on the fireplace.

OPPOSITE: Natural light and greenery create the feel of a garden inside a Dallas orangery designed by Cathy Kincaid with architecture by J. Wilson Fuqua.

OPPOSITE: A custom geometric rug by Doris Leslie Blau adds verve to a pink breakfast room designed by Bunny Williams in this Palm Beach retreat.

ABOVE: Set the scene—such as Amanda Lindroth did in this breakfast room with Swedish-inspired paneling. It gets a tropical touch with tieback slipcovers.

BREAKFAST ROOMS

ABOVE: Streamlined yet sculptural furniture ensures it's all about that view in a home designed by Thomas A. Kligerman, with interior design by Mia Jung.

LEFT: A table setting designed by Charlotte Moss, with lilac and other florals in a basket, looks simple—but is anything but.

OPPOSITE: This dining pavilion, designed by Anthony Baratta with architecture by Steve Giannetti, is a fantasy in blue and white.

ABOVE: Green and white china displayed in an open cabinet evokes the gardens beyond.

PAGES 168-169: A cheerful buck stands watchword over Hutton Wilkinson's kitchen and breakfast table.

OPPOSITE: An 18th-century French faience takes pride of place in a breakfast room designed by Cathy Kincaid.

Starry Ceilings

There's perhaps no more fitting place in the house than the breakfast room for a tented ceiling or fresco. After all, if things aren't looking up in the morning when you're well rested, when on earth will they? Take the opportunity to adorn the Fifth Wall, as it's called in the design industry, with lattice trelliage for graphic power. Or opt for a simple yet powerful statement: Paint the crown molding lime green and the actual ceiling a softer hue for a zingy playfulness that brightens any day. Call it your very own morning glory.

ABOVE: Botanical-print linen covers a set of Serge Roche–style chairs in designer Meg Braff's sunny Long Island, New York, breakfast room. "It makes you feel like you're sitting in the garden," she says.

OPPOSITE: Contemporary art by Zoë Pawlak adds a jolt of energy in a breakfast room by Alessandra Branca.

"I would concentrate on good use of mirrors and the incorporation of flowers. Whether the flowers are the real deal and placed around the room on plant stands or the two-dimensional variety that appear on fabrics or wallcoverings, it's a room that does well with vibrant colors and lots of light."

CELERIE KEMBLE, DESIGNER

OPPOSITE: Gracefully worn antiques and faux-distressed finishes create the feel of a European villa in a breakfast room designed by Laurie Steichen.

Seats with Style

Even a pretty-as-a-peony space can feel wilted if you're perched on a tired settee. Pick chairs with a shapely silhouette, something you'll happily camp out on for hours with your paper and Earl Grey. It's worth hunting down something iconic, though possibilities run the gamut. You could select mermaid-worthy painted shell-back antiques. Or echo Delft tiles on your walls with custom blue-and-white floral-upholstered side chairs adorned in nailhead trim. Or line one side of your breakfast table with a cherry-red, channel-tufted banquette that evokes the Americana of roadside diners. Even a simple flock of vintage rattan chairs can provide a pretty perch when whitewashed and softened with plush cushions in a cherry upholstery.

ABOVE: A red and white breakfast nook and kitchen feel especially upbeat when surrounded by glass, white paint, and stone in a home designed by Celerie Kemble.

OPPOSITE: A collection of press-back chairs from antique stores outfits the narrow table designer Nathan Turner put together at Alisal Guest Ranch, a cattle ranch at the base of the Santa Ynez mountains in Santa Barbara, California wine country.

BREAKFAST ROOMS 177

CHAPTER SEVEN

Bedrooms

The ascendant starlets of Old Hollywood had a secret when it came to achieving beauty sleep: They slept in beauty.

To awake refreshed and renewed, they sagely stocked their chambers with maximalist headboards, cocooning canopies, downy bed linens that swaddled them like a maternal embrace—all converging to create restful nights nonpareil. It's no wonder that today's designers opt for equally cinematic environs in the bedroom, arguably the most important space in the home for its ability to both transport us to worlds unknown (in our REM dreams) and help us emerge fresh from the chrysalis each morning. A canopy bed has a cozy effect, hung with embroidered cotton sateen on the interior, with greige silk flanking the exterior, cloaking you in quiet as you drift off to dreamland. Or hand-painted wallpaper and fretwork shutters that transform an urban bedroom into a hidden garden. Occasionally, the functional becomes bewitching, such as brilliant-white mosquito netting to keep unwelcome flighty callers at bay, or outsized mirrors to enlarge a room in an instant while reflecting the plush white-on-white dreamscape. Whatever your approach, keep maximizing your R&R top of mind: If a kitchen is the heart of the home, a bedroom is the happy.

PAGES 178-179: A large custom mirror makes this Charlotte, North Carolina, master bedroom designed by Betsy Brown feel even larger.

OPPOSITE: Panels of draperies on a four-post bed in a 17th-century Connecticut country house designed by Brooke and Steve Giannetti make it as coddling as a swaddle.

ABOVE: A painted antique iron bed makes magic in this master bedroom designed by Frank de Biasi on Long Island's North Shore.

LEFT: Designer Meg Braff selected an unexpected Serge Roche–inspired four poster with neo-baroque lines for this Long Island home.

OPPOSITE: A lavender sofa provides the ultimate winding-down respite when placed at the foot of the bed in this Aspen home by Texas designer J. Randall Powers.

Luxe Linens

Designers of late have been of one mind when it comes to dressing the bed: more is more is more. The simple and streamlined look that reigned in the early aughts has been disposed of in favor of blousy bed skirts and pristine monogrammed linens. Rising to find yourself cloaked in softness and splendor, once the extravagance of monarchs, is for anyone. And it's a lot more than thread count (though that certainly, well, counts). To assemble the ultimate berth, mull pairing scallop-edged boudoir pillows with a divergent graphic bed skirt or topping a pair of bunks with the same playful blue-and-white hand-blocked Indian cotton print that veils the walls. And don't forget the flounces. When it comes to good old-fashioned cocooning, nothing says cozy—or feels quite as swooningly romantic—like acres of tassels, ruffles, pleats, and trims, especially in a pretty bedroom, where it is imperative to furnish deliciously sweet dreams.

ABOVE: The walls of Hutton Wilkinson's Malibu guesthouse are covered in custom hand-blocked Indian cotton to match the bedspreads.

OPPOSITE: Go wild with pattern in lesser-used guest rooms to make a statement, as Mark D. Sikes did in this Alabama home.

ABOVE: In design duo Brooke and Steve Giannetti's Ojai, California, master retreat, sumptuous furnishings are balanced by bare white walls that emphasize the surrounding landscape.

PAGES 186–187: In a New England master bedroom by architect Thomas A. Kligerman with design by Mia Jung, an expansive window offers a panoramic view of the landscape, while a throw blanket that evokes Irish Aran Islands sweaters keeps things snug. "Everything is meant to echo where the sky meets the water and the water meets the land," says Kligerman.

ABOVE: Allowing window treatments to puddle supplies a space—this one in Santa Barbara, California, designed by Ann Holden—with old-world grandeur.

LEFT: Linen curtains and a white-on-white envelope of a room designed by Veere Grenney force the eye outdoors and into the lushness of Mustique beyond the terrace.

"Add beauty to your life every day with small touches, such as fresh peonies, roses, and ranunculus, especially in white or pink; having a signature candle—my favorite, Libertine by SOH Melbourne, is an under-the-radar scent that evokes orange blossoms and twigs; and of course, monograms. All of these gestures spark joy."

PALOMA CONTRERAS, DESIGNER

OPPOSITE: Antiques, such as an 18th-century English chair, give Richard Hallberg's Montecito, California, guest bedroom staying power.

ABOVE: Designer Phoebe Howard opted for whimsy in a surprising place—this custom pineapple-top four-post bed—for even more impact in this Palm Beach home.

RIGHT: Designer Katie Ridder layered orchid bed upholstery over cobalt blue grass cloth walls in this Hamptons home, with architecture by her husband, Peter Pennoyer. "Peter's classical architecture really frees me to do things that are vibrant and interesting" she says.

PAGES 192-193: Comfort doesn't mean a lack of aesthetic discipline, such as in this Aspen bedroom designed by Victoria Hagan.

ABOVE: A faux-fur throw can cozy up a clean-lined master bedroom, as in this retreat in architect Bobby McAlpine's Atlanta home. The distinct ceiling height creates theatrical tension. "The compression of low ceilings exaggerates the other lofty heights," McAlpine says. The resulting feeling, he explains, is one of "being held and released."

LEFT: The master bed in William Eubanks's 1920s Memphis cottage is canopied with green herringbone velvet, bringing in a connection to the emerald gardens beyond the window.

In a bedroom, it's vitally important to create moments of restful beauty for wherever the eye lands.

OPPOSITE: In a Southern California master bedroom designed by Laurie Steichen, gilded moldings echo the finish of the bed's corona, hewn from an antique French altar fragment.

ABOVE LEFT: In a Manhattan master bedroom designed by Ashley Whittaker, walls in hemp wallcovering give a whispery bit of texture.

ABOVE RIGHT: Monogram linens and a playful headboard set a lively tone in a Windsor, Florida, guest room designed by Alessandra Branca.

ABOVE: Hand-painted Gracie wallpaper and fretwork on shutters transform design historian Maureen Footer's New York City bedroom into a magical garden.

RIGHT: Mosquito nets, in brilliant white to match the antique linens, protect guests from unwelcome nocturnal visitors in this Mustique villa by Veere Grenney.

OPPOSITE: Golden accents and charming floral fabrics enliven architect James Carter's Birmingham, Alabama, bedroom.

Bedside Beauty

It's often the last thing you see before sleeping and the first thing you spy upon waking. It's not your spouse; it's your nightstand. And if you have any hope of starting your day, as the tired maxim puts it, on the right side of the bed, it had better be divine. To start, ensure you have the fussy basics: a carafe of filtered water, a delicious book, and a nosegay of fresh-cut blooms. Designers in the know take it a step further by injecting a dose of history: selecting antique side tables that evoke the storied splendor of house museums, or adding an object, like a Chinese foo dog, that conjures dreamy travels to faraway lands. Keep the look calm by corralling the functional (alarm clocks, notepads) in a gleaming tray for a tidy, serene look. And by all means, leave the phones in the other room—so you can rest for success.

ABOVE: Matching curtains and canopy in this Palm Beach suite envelop the master bedroom in glamour.

OPPOSITE: Antique suitcases make a statement when stacked in designer Susan Ferrier's Atlanta Tudor.

ABOVE: More is more is more: A favorite Rose Cumming floral dresses William Eubanks's guest bedroom walls, windows, and furniture in his 1920s Memphis home. "It's like the garden has come inside. It's a wonderful place to have your coffee and write your letters," Eubanks says. "I love rooms that wrap their arms around you."

OPPOSITE: A carafe of water at your bedside, such as in this Windsor, Florida, room by Alessandra Branca, makes you feel like a treasured guest in your own home.

"The key to a beautiful bedroom is two things: lighting and texture. Texture is the quilted matelassé on the bed, the folded linen duvet—all the feel-good things. Texture feels good, but lighting...lighting makes you look good."

STEPHANIE SABBE, DESIGNER

OPPOSITE: In this Nashville home designed by Stephanie Sabbe, sheer draperies at the window give the light an especially ethereal quality.

ABOVE: In a New England master bedroom by architect Thomas A. Kligerman with design by Mia Jung, an expansive window offers a panoramic view of the landscape, while a throw blanket that evokes Irish Aran Islands sweaters keeps things snug. "Everything is meant to echo where the sky meets the water and the water meets the land," says Kligerman.

ABOVE: Soft blues temper neutrals in a Dallas master suite designed by Cathy Kincaid.

LEFT: Designer and event planner Antony Todd created his New York City master bedroom in an alcove with ombré curtains. Crimson peonies add rich color to the muted, tonal room. "I love packing a vase with lots of stems of a single flower," Todd says. "It feels so luxurious."

BEDROOMS 207

ABOVE: A scalloped edge on a canopy bed in an Alabama home designed by Mark D. Sikes adds a touch of whimsy to an otherwise streamlined piece.

RIGHT: A reptilian-finish nightstand supplies a bedroom in Nicola and Elda Fabrizio's Italian home with exotic texture in an unlikely locale.

PAGES 208-209: A soft gray-and-white palette creates a tranquil mood in this Connecticut master bedroom by Timothy Whealon.

ABOVE: Burnished gold touches enrich a master bedroom designed by Ellie Cullman and architect John B. Murray.

LEFT: An antiqued mirrored wall and metallic accents give this Manhattan apartment designed by Jeffrey Bilhuber the glimmering allure of the cityscape beyond.

OPPOSITE: A fringed canopy gives off a palpably carefree mood in a Newport bedroom designed by Ruthie Sommers.

ABOVE: Hutton Wilkinson's master bedroom in Malibu brims with Chinese Chippendale pieces; the antique pagoda bed once belonged to the family of Winston Churchill's mother, Jennie Jerome Churchill.

"I often do a jewel on the hill, but this property demanded something more intimate that also fit the neighborhood. I wanted it to be a bit rambling. I wanted quirks. I wanted personality."

JAMES CARTER, ARCHITECT

OPPOSITE: James Carter's Birmingham, Alabama, bedroom is painted a rich green he calls both strong and cozy.

OPPOSITE: A brilliant silk jacquard showers a Provence, France, bedroom designed by Susan Bednar Long in florals, the bed trimmed in a lively coral sanguine silk.

ABOVE: The star of the show in designer Susan Ferrier's 1920s Atlanta Tudor: the 13-foot-tall bed curtains that accentuate an opulent headboard—and Piper, a rescue dog.

BEDROOMS 217

Frequent trips to the spa are a hallmark of CEOs and other kingpins for two reasons: When you feel good, you look good.

And when you look good, you triumph—both at work and in life. But you don't need a week of salve-rubbing and soul-scrubbing at The Alpina Gstaad. You need a bathroom that doubles as your own private fount of wellness. Devise a serene space—one where a pristine white-and-gray palette mimics the cleansing bubbles of sea foam, or a Moroccan retreat with a vaulted ceiling and flickering Moorish lanterns that's your own private hammam. Or line one wall in blonde woods to call to mind the alpine solace of a Finnish sauna, making sure to offset it with an airy light fixture. When in doubt, select something relaxing above all else and stock the room with a bounty of fresh bleached-white cotton towels, and you'll find yourself lingering in the room as you would at—well, a spa.

PAGES 218-219: A freestanding shimmering stainless steel-wrapped soaking tub in a Tel Aviv bath designed by Kevin Spearman becomes all the more tempting when installed atop a charmingly tiled floor. Art by Mary H. Case sets the tone: This is anything but bath time as usual.

OPPOSITE: Exotic Moroccan details, modern furniture, and classic Spanish Colonial architecture are blended in this Dallas home by architect Marc Appleton to create a home that is undeniably original.

OPPOSITE: In a Palm Beach bathroom, designer Phoebe Howard selected subtle flamingo-patterned wallpaper to nod to the tropical setting. Adding a simple skirt to the tub-side antique chair dresses it up the perfect amount.

ABOVE: Glass ceilings and walls provide the feeling of bathing alfresco in Brooke and Steve Giannetti's Ojai, California, house, which is set on four-and-a-half acres of undulant meadows and pastures.

Soaking Tubs to Love

The most exquisite hotel suites in the world have two things in common: butlers and soaking tubs. Install the latter in your bathroom and your scrub time will have an aura of a frothy vacation in Saint-Tropez, every single day. For the most bewitching bath, opt for a tub that stands alone, whether in a traditional space flanked by antiques or a sleek, modern one where free-flowing sheer curtains add drama. Then treat it as Jeeves might, filling it with 100°F bubbles, dotting the surface with a trail of garden rose petals, and steeping in it at your leisure. Candles optional.

ABOVE: A hand-painted mural by Jean Horihara Design gives this Art Deco powder room—in a storied Los Angeles home with an architectural renovation by Kevin A. Clark and design by Madeline Stuart—subtle glamour. Magic, it seems, is not just for the movies.

OPPOSITE: Antique terra-cotta tile puts the bath on firm footing in this Provence home designed by Susan Bednar Long.

ABOVE: A floral-relief installation by Nina Helms decorates the walls and ceilings of a Park Avenue bathroom designed by Thomas Pheasant. "There's a comfort in history, and yet this isn't about reproducing the past," the designer says. "It is about evolving geometry and essential relationships to strike a chord of, 'Oh, yes, I recognize this, but...wow, this is different!'"

OPPOSITE: A carved Indian archway provides a grand entrée into Hutton Wilkinson's guesthouse bath in Malibu. It cements one of Wilkinson's purposes for the farm, which is that it be a respite. A big night at the lodge—where there is no cell-phone reception or Internet—doesn't mean galas and gowns. It means gazing at "every star and constellation in the universe," Wilkinson says. Humanity first.

"In our travels, there are few critters left behind. They commemorate places we've been and have become part of a tribe that we love dearly."

BOBBY MCALPINE, ARCHITECT

OPPOSITE: A simple sink can be a piece of art, such as in architect Bobby McAlpine's Atlanta powder room, presided over by a Venetian bird sculpture purchased at the Antiques at the Gardens show at the Birmingham Botanical Gardens.

ABOVE: Baskets keep towels tidy and evoke the orderliness of a day spa in this Windsor, Florida, retreat by Alessandra Branca.

OPPOSITE: A romantic silk wallpaper by De Gournay echoes blue-gray tones throughout a historic Virginia house designed by Suzanne Kasler.

Mirror Image

Whether you spend hours preening before the looking glass or allow mere seconds for inspection, it's vital for self-esteem to set up a mirror that reflects you at your best. The most flattering type is that used by Dolly Parton and other honky-tonk luminaries: the Hollywood Mirror, bedecked by multiple opaque incandescent bulbs. Get a more discreet glamorizing effect by placing a sconce on either side of the mirror (ghastly shadows, begone!). By all means, pick a mirror with an artful frame that you'll enjoy looking at—such as a gilded and black chinoiserie stunner—lest you turn into that all-too-often imploring Evil Queen from *Snow White*. You are the fairest in the land; you don't need to ask.

ABOVE: A guest bath's custom vanity is topped with Crema Marfil marble in designer Betsy Shiverick's Palm Beach home.

OPPOSITE: Selecting an unexpected finish, such as this onyx counter in a Naples, Florida, powder room by Suzanne Kasler, is a lesson in everyday luxury.

OPPOSITE: A custom bubble chandelier adds a fanciful note to a minimalist master bath in Aspen designed by Victoria Hagan, with architecture by Joeb Moore. The soft, pale hues interact in miraculous ways with the blinding outside light. "It seems a lot whiter than it is," Hagan says. "It's actually full of color, and the sun reflecting off the snow gives those shades a life of their own."

ABOVE: In Dan Fink and Thomas O'Brien's Bellport, Long Island, retreat, the office bathroom features cork wall tiles.

CHAPTER NINE

Passages

It has been said, if you are unsure where you are going, any road can take you there. And that's right, of course.

Often neglected and the very last space to be decorated in any home, hallways should be front and center for all the use they get. Make yours more transportive than a simple pass-through: Line the walls in intricate shellwork for a jaw-dropping promenade, or hire a muralist to paint them with trompe l'oeil to mirror the stately manors of Buckinghamshire, England. If the hall contains any superfluous square footage, consider it your invitation to create a bonus space tailor-made for your passions, whether it's retreating with the latest thriller or catching up with your correspondence at a well-stocked antique desk. After all, this is where life actually happens—in the Chutes and Ladders. As they say—for good reason— it's not the destination, it's the journey.

PAGES 236-237: An open bronze and glass staircase set against custom oak-plank-paneled walls allows the architecture and the vistas beyond to shine in this dramatic Aspen getaway by architect Joeb Moore. It was designed around a series of small landings so "at any point," the home's designer, Victoria Hagan, says, "you can stop for a moment and enjoy the breathtaking view."

OPPOSITE: Shell-encrusted panels by Thomas Boog gloriously mimic wallpaper in a Palm Beach home by Sarah Ramsey and Claire Ratliff of Cullman & Kravis.

ABOVE: An antique Flemish tapestry steals the show in an airy central staircase in a Provence farmhouse with interiors by Bunny Williams and remodeled architecture by Norman Davenport Askins. "Every project is like a new romance," Williams says. "I stay up at night thinking about it."

OPPOSITE: A 19th-century alabaster sculpture adds a moment of passing beauty in Dan Fink and Thomas O'Brien's Bellport, Long Island, stair hall. "These rooms are about time—current and past," says O'Brien. "There's so much about today that doesn't have that character."

OPPOSITE: A latticework hallway in writer and designer Sara Ruffin Costello's New Orleans home.

ABOVE: A pair of pink perches bring a dose of fun to this southwest Florida entry by Suzanne Kasler, with Venetian plaster walls for soft iridescence. The floor is white limestone "embedded with miniature seashells," says Kasler.

ABOVE: "The details of everyday life are the soul of a house," says designer Betsy Brown, who hung puddling curtains in this simple Charlotte, North Carolina, hallway to heavenly effect.

OPPOSITE: This monochromatic Washington, D.C., entry hall by Thomas Pheasant has a polished audacity, with contemporary art and furniture placed within a classical envelope. Says the client: "Tom's clean lines and neutral colors make me feel at peace."

"Hallways are often neglected in the decor department because they're seen as a means to an end, a way to get from room to room. However, I pay special attention to them just for that reason. Hallways are a moment for a beautiful piece of art that you love and will be able to enjoy and see when you walk through every day."

TIMOTHY WHEALON, DESIGNER

OPPOSITE: A creamy palette and spare furnishings showcase the sculptural architecture of a Virginia home designed by Suzanne Kasler, with architecture by Madison Spencer.

ABOVE: Wide-plank pine floors and a Dutch door recall the heritage of an 1801 Hamptons, Long Island, house with interior design by Sharon Simonaire.

OPPOSITE: The fanciful overdoor at Amanda Lindroth's Palm Beach apartment was painted by artist Aldous Bertram based on the plaster chinoiserie version at Claydon House in England.

OPPOSITE: Subtle graphic lines create a tailored frame for the wild beyond the windows in this seafront abode by architect Tom Kligerman.

ABOVE: In this whimsical West Palm Beach abode by designer Lars Bolander, an open-air entry leads to both the main house and its tropical gardens for fresh, breezy flow.

Gallery Walls

Your grandparents in their wedding garb. That euphoric trip to Montserrat. The baby, toddling as a warbler in the dew-dotted grass. Occasionally, in this Instagrammed world, only a picture can do justice to memory, and hallways are the loveliest place to hang them. Here, they won't clutter a countertop but rather remind you of each moment as you pass. This is also the place to hang your collections of ephemera, such as architectural drawings—your own personal Louvre Museum, at the ready for contemplation.

ABOVE: Architectural drawings are hung salon-style in architect James Carter's Birmingham, Alabama, hallway, providing a visual feast.

OPPOSITE: Designer Katie Leede designed her Soho, New York, entryway with a bold note—Farrow & Ball's Arsenic paint color. "A strong personal style doesn't necessarily require a big budget," says Leede, "but it does require a certain élan—zip, oomph, verve."

ABOVE: Distilled to its essence, geometry elevates everyday destinations and passages, such as in this master foyer on Park Avenue designed by Thomas Pheasant. "What captivated me the minute I walked in," he says, "was the wonderful natural light on all sides. That's a luxury you can't fake. It's either there or it isn't."

OPPOSITE: In the upstairs landing of an Alabama home designed by Mark D. Sikes, a mash-up of patterns—checks, florals, and stripes—is surprisingly soothing thanks to its restricted palette.

Adorn your hallways with art, fresh flowers, curated antiques, or a cozy runner underfoot. Why not make your travels as five-star as possible?

OPPOSITE: Richard Hallberg's rooms in his Montecito home, such as this hall with an original wood staircase with 14-inch-tall treads, aren't decorated so much as they are a repository for cherished things that have been pulled together over a lifetime. "This is not truly a design job," the designer says. "It's an assemblage of things that I've acquired over the decades, all meant to feel like they've been here for years."

ABOVE LEFT: Any quiet corner can create a moment of reprieve, such as this antique desk and stool in the front entry hall of Michael DePerno and Andrew Fry's 1910 Connecticut cottage.

ABOVE RIGHT: Persian-inspired wallpaper adds quiet, subtle pattern to a circa-1860 Connecticut entry hall designed by Timothy Whealon.

"A hallway is a blank canvas. As long as it's woven together conceptually in some way, shape or form, it will be beautiful. The obvious way to decorate it is with a collection of something."

TAMMY CONNOR, DESIGNER

OPPOSITE: A quiet mural in an entrance hall designed by Tammy Connor, painted by Scott Waterman, was inspired by Central Park.

ABOVE: An Upper East Side entry hall designed by Nick Olsen reverberates with geometric patterns. "These homeowners are really vivid and animated people," he says. "They love to express themselves."

LEFT: An antique Chinese elm bench can turn any few square feet into a mudroom, such as in this side entrance of Michael DePerno and Andrew Fry's Connecticut cottage.

OPPOSITE: Swedish cabinets and 18th-century urns turn a Santa Barbara, California, central hallway designed by Ann Holden into an art gallery.

Grace Underfoot

Hallways are devoted to transporting you—quickly and easily—from one space to another innumerable times a day. So why not make the actual path as dreamy as possible? Lackluster carpeting just won't do to get you where you're going. You might contemplate sourcing salvaged French parquet floorboards for a timeworn effect that creates a literal track to glory, even in a new build, or installing the classic checkerboard in polished marble in a nod to the Galleria Grande in the 17th-century Palace of Venaria in Piedmont region of Italy.

ABOVE: The parquet flooring in this North Shore, Long Island, stair hall designed by Frank de Biasi is from a Paris flea market. "They don't mind things that are a little worn or don't match," de Biasi says. "Everything has a patina—or soon will acquire one, with the amount of use this house gets."

OPPOSITE: An antique settee pops when juxtaposed with graphic wallcovering in this Alabama entry hall designed by Mark D. Sikes. "From the time I was in college, I've always been on the hunt for antiques. I bought what I loved and then figured out what to do with it later," says homeowner Ragan Cain.

OPPOSITE: A deep-purple envelope allows shapely furniture and accessories to pop in this Celerie Kemble–designed hallway on Park Avenue. "I'm always exploring fresh inspiration," she says. "I get itchy to use ideas that feel new to me."

ABOVE: For dramatic impact, designer Amanda Lindroth sheathed a foyer in mint-colored treillage. The breezy, colorful take on classic Bahamian style rivals the enchantment of Slim Aarons's vintage photographs of glamorous island life.

INDEX

Page references of photos indicate location of captions.

A

Aarons, Slim, 265
Agave salmiana, 86
Alfresco baths, 223
Alfresco entertaining
    about: possibilities for, 94
    on docks, 105
    fireplaces, 90
    lighting, 98
    on porches, 74
    seating, 94, 100
    table settings, 105

Alisal Guest Ranch (California), 176
Allfree, Andrew, 19
Ancient Egyptians, 74
Antique and vintage items
    in bedrooms, 190
    in breakfast rooms, 174
    hunt for, 176, 262
    lighting fabricated from, 122
    in living rooms, 26
    modern features mixed with, 19, 26, 44, 46
    pale walls for setting off, 20
    pottery, 130
    prints, 33, 51, 64
    suitcases, 200
    tableware, 130
    wrought-iron furniture, 64, 183

Appleton, Marc, 141, 220
Art deco style, 73, 224
Artwork
    about: as conversation pieces, 40
    for adding depth to rooms, 44, 49
    in breakfast rooms, 172
    for bringing the outside in, 22
    color palettes based on, 33, 252
    designer-made, 48
    firewood as, 26
    frames for, 19, 54
    as living room centerpiece, 16, 40, 48, 54

    in passages, 240, 252, 261
    tapestries and textiles as, 40, 54, 144, 240
    vintage and antique prints, 33, 51, 64

Askins, Norman Davenport, 240
Aubusson tapestry, 144

B

Baccarat glassware, 54
Baratta, Anthony, 158, 167
Bar cabinets, 54
Barn door, for hiding TV, 26
Baths, 218–235
    about: mirrors as focal points, 232; possibilities for, 220
    arched entry, 226
    Art deco style, 224
    ceiling designs, 223, 226
    flooring, 220, 224
    glass walls and ceiling, 223
    guest baths, 226, 232
    lighting, 235
    mirrors as focal points, 232
    monochromatic scheme for, 230
    Moroccan motif, 220
    murals, 224
    office baths, 235
    powder rooms, 224, 228, 232
    sculptures as focal points, 228
    seating, 223
    sinks, 228, 232
    soaking tubs, 220
    towel storage, 230
    wall coverings, 223, 226, 230, 235

Bedrooms, 178–217
    about: bed linens, 184, 204; lighting, 204; nightstands, 200; possibilities for, 180
    accent colors, 183, 195, 198, 207, 211, 214
    bed curtains, 180, 198, 217
    bed linens: accent colors, 198; fabric patterns, 9, 184, 188, 198, 202, 217; matching wall coverings to, 184, 194, 202; monogrammed, 190, 197; Provençal style, 217; texture variations, 195, 198, 204, 206
    bedside tables, 200, 202, 210
    canopy beds, 9, 180, 195, 200, 210, 213
    ceiling height, 195
    Chinese-inspired furniture in, 213
    collections featured in, 200
    flower arrangements, 190, 207
    four-poster beds, 183, 194
    headboard styles, 197, 217
    iron beds, 183
    mirrors as focal points, 180, 197, 211
    moldings, 197
    mosquito netting, 198
    pale hues, 210
    Provençal style, 217
    seating, 183, 190
    in studios, 207
    with views, 188, 195, 206
    wall coverings, 194, 197, 211
    window treatments, 189, 198, 200, 204

Bilhuber, Jeffrey, 211
Blau, Doris Leslie, 165
Board-and-batten walls, 19
Bolander, Lars, 107, 251
Boog, Thomas, 50
Bougainvillea, 94
Bouyoucos, Carol Greenan, 22
Boxwood
    hedges, 80
    as iconic plant, 86
    potted, 83, 98

Braff, Meg, 172, 183
Branca, Alessandra
    bath by, 230
    bedrooms by, 197, 202
    breakfast room by, 172
    dining room by, 132
    kitchen by, 152
    living rooms by, 33, 44

Breakfast rooms, 160–177
    about: ceiling designs, 172; flower arrangements, 174; mirrors as focal points, 174; possibilities for, 162; seating, 176

accent colors, 167, 170, 176
artwork, 172
European villa style, 174
fabric choices, 162, 165, 172
faux finishes, 174
flooring, 165
flower arrangements, 167, 174
houseplants, 162
kitchens linked to, 170
lighting, 162
paneling, 165
Provençal style, 162, 170
sculptural furniture, 167
Swedish-inspired, 165
table settings, 167
tiled walls, 162

Brown, Betsy
bedroom by, 180
living rooms by, 14, 44
passage by, 244
sunroom by, 73

Burbank, Luther, 114
Bustamante, Luis, 49, 143
Butler's pantry, 122

C

Cain, Ragan, 262
Carter, Darryl, 26, 144
Carter, James, 51, 198, 214, 252
Case, Mary H., 220
Ceiling designs
baths, 223, 226
breakfast rooms, 172
dining rooms, 131, 142
kitchens, 152
living rooms, 33, 39
sunrooms, 70, 77

Chairs. *See* Occasional chairs
Chandeliers, 130, 162, 235
Château de Montigny-sur-Avre, 19
Chelsea Editions fabric, 131
Chinese-inspired furniture, 213
Churchill, Jennie Jerome, 213
Cicero, Marcus Tullius, 80
Clark, Kevin A., 73, 224
Classicism, 66
Claydon House, 248
Collections
in bedrooms, 200
in dining rooms, 141
hunt for, 156, 176, 262

in kitchens, 151, 156
in living rooms, 17, 31

Connor, Tammy, 51, 58, 258
Conservatories, 66
Consoles, 22
Contreras, Paloma, 190
Cordsen, Kate, 44, 74
Costello, Sara Ruffin, 243
Countertops, 148, 151, 158
Creeping fig, 80
Crema Marfil marble, 232
Cullman, Ellie, 19, 211
Cullman & Kravis, 238
Cumming, Rose, 202
Curtains. *See* Window treatments
Cypress trees, 80, 86

D

Daffodils, 102
Dahlias, 102
De Biasi, Frank, 183, 262
Dedar fabrics, 54
De Gournay, 230
DePerno, Michael
dining room by, 135
living room by, 52
passages by, 257, 261
sunroom by, 64

Derian, John, 64, 124
De Rothschild, Marie-Hélène, 112
Dining rooms, 110–145. *See also* Alfresco entertaining; Breakfast rooms
about: lighting, 138; possibilities for, 112; tablescapes, 124
accent colors, 115, 132, 138, 143
bold color scheme, 118
ceiling designs, 131, 143
collections featured in, 141
custom plasterwork, 141
flooring, 143
flower arrangements, 135, 141
formal approach to, 116
hand-painted walls, 112, 124, 135
lighting, 115, 118, 122, 130, 138
mirrors as focal points, 127
monochromatic scheme, 112, 114, 122, 132
Moroccan motif, 141
pale hues, 116
paneling, 135
seating, 122, 135
table centerpieces, 118

tablescapes, 124, 127, 132, 138, 144
tapestries, 144
window treatments, 131

Dixon, D. Stanley, 22, 115
Draperies. *See* Window treatments

E

Eating areas. *See* Alfresco entertaining; Breakfast rooms; Dining rooms
Entry halls, 244, 251, 257, 261, 262
Eubanks, William, 80, 94, 195, 202

F

Fabrizio, Elda and Nicola, 54, 155, 210
Farrow & Ball, 252
Fatio, Maurice, 107
Ferrier, Susan, 200, 217
Fig trees, 92
Fink, Dan, 54, 92, 235, 240
Flooring
in baths, 220, 224
in breakfast rooms, 165
in dining rooms, 143
in kitchens, 148, 151
in passages, 243, 248, 262
in sunrooms, 66, 77

Florian Schulz lighting, 51
Flower arrangements. *See also* Gardens
in bedrooms, 190, 207
in breakfast rooms, 167, 174
in dining rooms, 135, 141
feral beauty of, 9

Footer, Maureen, 31, 59, 144, 198
Fountains, 84, 92, 102
Foyers, 254, 265
French doors, 74
French gilt mirror, 38
Fry, Andrew
dining room by, 135
living room by, 52
passages by, 257, 261
sunroom by, 64

Fuqua, J. Wilson, 70, 162

G

Garden room, as TV room, 26
Gardens, 78–109. *See also* Alfresco entertaining; *specific plants and trees*
    about: iconic plantings, 86; outdoor living spaces, 100; possibilities for, 80; secret garden places, 84
    arbors, 80, 98, 102, 105, 107
    entrances, 92
    fireplaces, 90
    focal points, 83
    formal style, 80, 83
    fountains, 84, 92, 102
    indoor-outdoor spaces, 90, 92, 105, 107
    lighting, 98
    neutral palette, 98
    partitioning of, 94
    ponds, 84
    pool areas, 86
    potted plants, 83, 90, 92, 98
    potting areas, 91
    Provençal style, 80, 98
    seating areas, 86, 90, 94, 98, 100
    trellises, 94
    vegetable garden, 107
    walled gardens, 92

George III side tables, 26
Giannetti, Brooke and Steve
    bath by, 223
    bedrooms by, 180, 188
    breakfast room by, 167
    dining room by, 143
    garden by, 107
    kitchen by, 158

Green, Susan Zises, 33, 77, 107, 114
Grenney, Veere, 86, 122, 189, 198
Guest baths, 226, 232. *See also* Baths
Guillot, Perry, 80

H

Hadley, Albert, 5, 6, 9
Hagan, Victoria
    bath by, 235
    bedroom by, 194
    kitchen by, 158
    living room by, 58
    passage by, 238

Hallberg, Richard, 84, 190, 257
Hallways, 262
Happy cabinet liners, 150

Harris, Steven, 49
Heisey glassware, 54
Helms, Nina, 226
Holden, Ann, 40, 83, 189, 261
Horihara, Jean, 224
Houseplants, 66
Howard, Jim, 148
Howard, Phoebe, 16, 194, 223

I

Ireland, Kathryn M., 98
Irises, 102
Iron-cased windows, 66
Ivy, 80

J

Japanese textiles, 54
Jung, Mia, 38, 167, 188, 206

K

Kalachnikoff, Nadine, 107
Kasler, Suzanne
    baths by, 230, 232
    dining room by, 122
    passages by, 243, 246

Kemble, Celerie, 174, 176, 265
Kincaid, Cathy
    bedroom by, 207
    breakfast rooms by, 162, 170
    sunrooms by, 62, 70, 77, 162

Kitchens, 146–159
    about: backsplashes, 152; collections, 156; countertops, 158; possibilities for, 148
    accent colors, 155, 156
    backsplashes, 158
    breakfast rooms linked to, 170
    cabinets, 151, 155
    ceiling designs, 152
    collections featured in, 151, 156
    countertops, 148, 151, 158
    flooring, 148, 151
    interior drawers, 155
    islands, 148, 151, 152
    lighting, 152, 156
    Louis XV style, 158
    monochromatic scheme, 155
    Provençal style, 156
    simplicity of, 158
    texture variations, 148
    white features, 155

Kligerman, Thomas A.
    bedrooms by, 188, 206
    breakfast room by, 167
    living room by, 38
    passage by, 251
    sunroom by, 70

Kumquat trees, 66

L

Lafourcade, Alexandre, 66
Landings, 238, 254
Landscaping architecture. *See* Gardens
Langham, Richard Keith, 10, 31, 51
Latticework wallpaper and wall coverings, 62, 172, 243, 265
Leede, Katie, 252
Levens Hall, 86
Libertine candles, 190
Libraries, 19, 31, 51
Lighting
    for alfresco entertaining, 98
    for baths, 235
    for bedrooms, 204
    for breakfast rooms, 162
    for dining rooms, 115, 118, 122, 130, 138
    fabricated from antique items, 122
    for kitchens, 152, 156
    for living rooms, 51

Lilies, 102
Limestone floors, 66, 151, 243
Lindroth, Amanda
    breakfast room by, 165
    dining room by, 138
    passages by, 248, 265

Living rooms, 12–59
    about: artwork as conversation pieces, 40; occasional chairs, 20, 26; possibilities for, 14
    antiques mixed with modern features, 19, 26, 44, 46
    artwork, for adding depth, 44, 49
    artwork, as centerpiece, 16, 40, 48, 54
    bar cabinet, 54
    bold color scheme, 5, 19, 59
    candles, 44
    ceiling designs, 33, 39
    collections featured in, 17, 31
    fireplaces, 40
    firewood as art in, 26
    hiding electronics, 26
    high-gloss paint for, 31, 39

Japanese-inspired, 44
as libraries, 19, 31, 51
lighting, 51
listening nooks, 52
mirrors as focal points, 14, 38
moldings, 17, 58
monochromatic scheme, 26
neutral palette, 48, 52, 58
occasional chairs, 20, 26, 51
pale hues, 20, 22, 32, 33, 39
paneling, 19, 32, 38, 51, 54
partitioning options, 32, 44, 54, 58
plaster walls, 48
sculptural furniture, 20
shelving customized, 31
tapestries for, 40, 54
texture variations, 16, 19, 48, 52, 59
throw pillows, 16, 54
timeless design for, 5
trees featured in, 52
with views, 38, 58
white features, 54
window seats, 39
window treatments, 22, 59

Loggias, 74, 77, 107
Long, Susan Bednar
    bath by, 224
    bedroom by, 217
    dining rooms by, 130, 131

Lotus ponds, 84
Louis XV chairs, 14
Louis XVI chairs, 26

M

Malone, Carolyn, 22, 38, 115
Marble, 148
McAlpine, Bobby
    bath by, 228
    bedroom by, 195
    on color, 98
    dining room by, 122
    garden by, 98
    living room by, 54

M. Carbine Restorations, 148
McBride, Nate, 33
Metropolitan Opera, 138
Meyers, Nancy, 148
Mirrors
    in baths, 232
    in bedrooms, 180, 197, 211
    in breakfast rooms, 174
    in dining rooms, 127
    in living rooms, 14, 38

Molyneux, Juan Pablo, 14, 83, 135
Monet, Claude, 107
Monpoint, Frédéric, 135
Moore, Joeb, 58, 158, 235, 238
Moss, Charlotte, 167
Murals, 131, 224, 258
Murray, John B., 19, 211
Mus, Jean, 100

N

Narcissi, 102
Nevins, Deborah, 107
Newman, Suzanne, 31
Nisbet, Amanda, 32, 39, 156

O

O'Brien, Thomas, 54, 92, 235, 240
Occasional chairs, 14, 20, 26, 51
Oetgen, John, 19, 62
Olive trees, 86
Olsen, Nick, 52, 66, 261
Orangery, 66, 70, 162
Outdoor spaces. See Alfresco
    entertaining; Gardens
Owners' collections. See Collections

P

Palace of Venaria (Italy), 262
Paneling
    in breakfast rooms, 165
    contrasting furniture for, 54
    crewel panel, 10
    in dining rooms, 135
    embroidered, 51
    in living rooms, 19, 32, 38, 51, 54
    weathered, 51

Papachristidis, Alex, 46, 124
Parish-Hadley, 5
Parlors, 14. See also Living rooms
Parquet flooring, 262
Passages, 236–265
    about: flooring, 262; possibilities for, 238, 246, 258
    accent colors, 243, 265
    artwork displays, 240, 252, 261
    curtains, 244
    doorways, 248
    entry halls, 244, 251, 257, 261, 262
    flooring, 243, 248, 262
    foyers, 254, 265
    geometric patterns, 254, 261
    hallways, 262
    landings, 238, 254
    monochromatic scheme, 244, 248
    murals, 258
    natural light, 254
    pale hues, 246
    Provençal style, 240
    seating, 243, 254, 261
    staircases, 238, 240, 246, 257
    stair halls, 262
    with views, 238, 251
    wall coverings, 238, 243, 254, 257, 265

Pawlak, Zoë, 172
Pennoyer, Peter, 194
Personal collections. See Collections
Pheasant, Thomas
    bath by, 226
    dining rooms by, 118, 130
    passages by, 244, 254

Pickford, Mary, 10, 51
Plank flooring, 248
Ponds, 84
Pools, 86
Powder rooms, 224, 228, 232.
    See also Baths
Powers, J. Randall, 152, 183
Public art, 40

R

Ramsey, Sarah, 238
Rath, Hans Harald, 138
Ratliff, Claire, 238
Rees, Tim, 98
Rheinstein, Suzanne, 44, 105
Ridder, Katie, 194
Robinson, Keith, 98, 105, 135
Roche, Serge, 172, 183
Roman marble corbel, 20
Roses, 80, 90, 102, 105
Rugs, 31, 58, 165

S

Sabbe, Stephanie, 204
Saladino, John, 20, 131, 151
Scented candles, 190
Screened porches, 62
Sculptural furniture, 20, 167
Sculptures
- in baths, 228
- busts, 31, 131
- as living room centerpiece, 48
- in passages, 240

Shiverick, Betsy, 16
Shrader, Scott
- fountain by, 92
- garden seating by, 100
- on gardens for living and entertaining, 84, 100
- large plantings by, 86
- outdoor dining spaces by, 91, 94
- outdoor fireplace by, 90

Side tables, 26, 200, 202, 210
Sikes, Mark D.
- bedrooms by, 184, 210
- on collections, 156
- dining room by, 112
- kitchen by, 150
- passages by, 254, 262
- sunroom by, 64

Sills, Stephen, 20, 151, 155
Simonaire, Sharon, 17, 248
Sitting areas. *See* Living rooms
SOH Melbourne, 190
Solarium. *See* Sunrooms
Sommers, Ruthie, 40, 138, 213
Spearman, Kevin, 59, 100, 220
Spencer, Madison, 246
Stainless steel cabinets, 151, 155
Staircases, 238, 240, 246, 257
Stair halls, 262
Steel-cased windows, 73
Steichen, Laurie, 148, 174, 197
Steuben glassware, 54
Stevens, Alecia, 33
Stuart, Madeline, 58, 73, 224
Sultanabad rug, 31
Summers, Emily, 141
Sunporches, 64, 74

Sunrooms, 60–77
- about: appeal of, 70; possibilities for, 62; wicker furniture, 74
- bold color scheme, 66
- ceiling designs, 70, 77
- flooring, 66, 77
- French doors, 74
- furniture options, 64, 74
- neutral palette, 73
- railings, 62
- texture variations, 70
- trellis-clad, 62
- white features, 73
- window treatments for, 64

Swarovski crystal starburst chandeliers, 138

T

Tablescapes, 124, 127, 132, 138, 144
Tapestries and textiles, 40, 54, 144, 240
Throw pillows, 16, 54
Todd, Antony, 22, 127, 207
Topiary, 66, 86, 90
Trellises, 94
Trellis wallpaper and wall coverings, 62, 172, 243, 265
Turner, Melanie, 115, 155
Turner, Nathan, 176
Twain, Mark, 66

U

Urns, 83, 261

V

Van den Thillart, Colette, 48, 92, 105
Van der Straeten, Hervé, 14
Vermeersch, Pieter, 49
Vintage items. *See* Antique and vintage items

W

Walled gardens, 92
Waterman, Scott, 258
Whealon, Timothy
- bedroom by, 210
- butler pantry by, 122
- dining room by, 143
- living room by, 39
- passage by, 257
- on passages, 246

Whittaker, Ashley, 22, 48, 197
Wicker furniture, 64, 74, 122
Wilkinson, Hutton
- bath by, 226
- bedrooms by, 184, 213
- breakfast room by, 170
- living room by, 17

Williams, Bunny
- breakfast rooms by, 162, 165
- dining room by, 127
- on gardens, 98
- living rooms by, 26, 32
- on one-of-a-kind items, 32
- passage by, 240

Windows
- as focal point, 58, 189
- iron-cased, 66
- steel-cased, 73

Window seats, 39
Window treatments
- bed curtains, 180, 198, 217
- in bedrooms, 189, 198, 200, 204
- bold statements made by, 40, 59, 189, 200
- in dining rooms, 131
- fabric patterns, 49, 64, 131
- in living rooms, 22, 59
- neutral palette, 22, 59, 204
- for partitioning rooms, 44, 207
- for sunrooms, 64

Winfrey, Oprah, 90, 102
Wrought iron furniture, 64, 183

PHOTOGRAPHY CREDITS

© MELANIE ACEVEDO: 30, 31 (2), 59, 78-79, 95, 145, 195, 198, 202, 253

© MALI AZIMA: 83, 115, 155

© ALEXANDRE BAILHACHE: 15, 66, 82, 128-129, 131, 134, 216, 225

© GORDON BEALL: 27, 144

© PAMELA COOK/STUDIO D: 170

© PAUL COSTELLO: 242

© ROGER DAVIES: 17, 81, 159, 166, 168-169, 184, 213, 227

© ERICA GEORGE DINES: 201, 217

© PETER FRANK EDWARDS: 4, 7

© MIGUEL FLORES-VIANNA: 63

© J. SAVAGE GIBSON: 16, 110-111, 194, 222

© TRIA GIOVAN: 107, 139, 165

© MAX KIM-BEE: 18, 19, 22 (2), 32, 39, 40, 48 (2), 49, 55, 58, 60-61, 72, 83, 85, 93, 104, 119, 127, 130, 143, 146-147, 149, 152, 154, 157, 175, 182, 183, 189, 191, 196, 197, 207, 210, 211, 224, 226, 245, 254, 256, 260, 262

© FRANCESCO LAGNESE: 11, 24-25, 28-29, 34, 51, 53, 54, 76, 92, 108, 114, 126, 164, 176, 235, 241, 261, 264

© THOMAS LOOF: 1, 20, 33, 42-43, 47, 105, 109, 125, 131, 133, 135, 151, 153, 173, 194, 197, 203, 211, 230, 251, 265

© JOSHUA MCHUGH: 67

© DAVID MEREDITH: 99

© JAMES MERRELL: 68-69, 77, 140, 141, 163, 171, 207, 221

© CHARLOTTE MOSS: 167

© PETER MURDOCK: 17, 21, 151, 155, 248

© AMY NEUNSINGER: 64, 113, 150, 185, 210, 255, 263

© DAVID OLIVER: 87, 123, 189, 198

© VICTORIA PEARSON: 88-89, 103, 114, 177

© ERIC PIASECKI: 239

© LAURA RESEN: 52, 65, 136-137, 257, 261

© LISA ROMEREIN: 44, 86, 90, 91 (2), 92, 94, 100, 105, 106, 107, 142, 181, 188, 223

© PAIGE RUMORE: 205

© LUCY SCHAEFFER: 124

© ANNIE SCHLECHTER: 12-13, 23, 38, 44, 51, 73, 115, 172, 178-179, 183, 199, 215, 244, 252

© KEVIN SPEARMAN DESIGN GROUP: 59, 101, 218-219

© SIMON UPTON: 2-3, 19, 50, 54, 58, 96-97, 120-121, 195, 229, 233, 243, 259

© JONNY VALIANT: 249

© MIKKEL VANG: 98

© FRITZ VON DER SCHULENBURG: 32, 98, 160-161, 240

© WILLIAM WALDRON: 36-37, 39, 41, 56-57, 71, 122, 138, 143, 158, 167, 186-187, 192-193, 206, 208-209, 212, 234, 236-237, 250, 258

© BJÖRN WALLANDER: 16, 35, 38, 45, 49, 74, 75, 116, 117, 122, 200, 231, 232, 247

© BRIAN WOODCOCK: 8, 64, 90, 141

HEARST HOME

Copyright © 2020 by
Hearst Magazine Media, Inc.

All rights reserved. The written instructions in this volume are intended for the personal use of the reader and may be reproduced for that purpose only. Any other use, especially commercial use, is forbidden under law without the written permission of the copyright holder.

Cover and book design by William van Roden

Library of Congress Cataloging-in-Publication Data Available on Request

10 9 8 7 6 5 4 3 2 1

Published by Hearst Home, an imprint of Hearst Books/Hearst Magazine Media, Inc.

Hearst Magazine Media, Inc.

300 West 57th Street
New York, NY 10019

Veranda, Hearst Home, the Hearst Home logo, and Hearst Books are registered trademarks of Hearst Magazine Media, Inc.

For information about custom editions, special sales, premium and corporate

Purchases: hearst.com/magazines/hearst-books

Printed in China

ISBN 978-1-950785-03-2